R C

This is the most famous of all Shakespeare's plays, first printed in 1597. It is a story of passionate young love, in the beautiful Italian city of Verona. Romeo and Juliet are the star-crossed lovers, who meet, fall in love, and promise to be true to each other for ever. A simple love story, with the saddest of all possible endings.

Love is strong, but not as strong as family tradition, or hate, or revenge. Like young people all over the world, Romeo and Juliet want the right to decide their future for themselves, but in the end the state and their families are too powerful for them. Romeo and Juliet cannot live without each other, and if they are not allowed to marry and live together, there is only one way out.

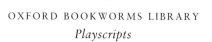

OXFORD BOOKWORMS LIBRARY

Playscripts

Romeo and Juliet

Stage 2 (700 headwords)

Playscripts Series Editor: Clare West

WILLIAM SHAKESPEARE

Romeo and Juliet

Retold by
Alistair McCallum

OXFORD UNIVERSITY PRESS

OXFORD
UNIVERSITY PRESS

Great Clarendon Street, Oxford OX2 6DP

Oxford University Press is a department of the University of Oxford.
It furthers the University's objective of excellence in research, scholarship,
and education by publishing worldwide in

Oxford New York

Auckland Cape Town Dar es Salaam Hong Kong Karachi
Kuala Lumpur Madrid Melbourne Mexico City Nairobi
New Delhi Shanghai Taipei Toronto

With offices in

Argentina Austria Brazil Chile Czech Republic France Greece
Guatemala Hungary Italy Japan Poland Portugal Singapore
South Korea Switzerland Thailand Turkey Ukraine Vietnam

OXFORD and OXFORD ENGLISH are registered trade marks of
Oxford University Press in the UK and in certain other countries

ISBN 978 0 19 423521 1

A complete recording of this Bookworms edition of
Romeo & Juliet is available on audio CD ISBN 978 0 19 423527 3

Printed in China

Photographs courtesy of BBC Picture Archives
from the television film *Romeo and Juliet* (1978)
Copyright © BBC 1978

For more information on the Oxford Bookworms Library,
visit www.oup.com/bookworms

CONTENTS

INTRODUCTION

Romeo and Juliet is a story about two families, the Montagues and the Capulets. It is set in Verona, a town in the north of Italy, over five hundred years ago. When the play begins, there has been an argument between these two families for many years.

PERFORMANCE NOTES

Act 1 Scene 1 and 2: A street in Verona
       Scene 3 and 4: The Capulets' house
Act 2 Scene 1: A garden outside the Capulets' house
       Scene 2: Father Lawrence's garden
       Scene 3: A street in Verona
       Scene 4: Father Lawrence's house
Act 3 Scene 1: A street in Verona
       Scene 2 and 5: Juliet's bedroom
       Scene 3: Father Lawrence's house
       Scene 4: The Capulets' house
Act 4 Scene 1: Father Lawrence's house
       Scene 2 and 4: The Capulets' house
       Scene 3: Juliet's bedroom
Act 5 Scene 1: A street in Mantua
       Scene 2: A garden outside a church

You will need some swords, a knife, glasses and bottles, tables and chairs, masks, a ring, gold coins, flowers, and some musical instruments.

CHARACTERS IN THE PLAY

The Montague family
Lord Montague
Lady Montague
Romeo, the Montagues' son
Benvolio, Romeo's cousin

The Capulet family
Lord Capulet
Lady Capulet
Juliet, the Capulets' daughter
Tybalt, Juliet's cousin

Other characters
Escalus, Prince of Verona
Paris, a friend of the Prince's
Mercutio, a friend of Romeo's
Juliet's Nurse
Father Lawrence, a priest
Father John, a friend of Father Lawrence's
People of Verona and Mantua
Lord Montague's servants
Lord Capulet's servants
Shopkeeper
Musicians

Romeo and Juliet

Trouble in Verona

A street in Verona, Italy. Some of Lord Montague's and Lord Capulet's servants are fighting and shouting.

LORD CAPULET'S SERVANTS We hate the Montagues! Capulet is a better lord than Montague!

LORD MONTAGUE'S SERVANTS We'll kill you for that! Death to the Capulets! (*Benvolio enters.*)

BENVOLIO What's happening? Stop! Stop fighting!
He tries to stop them, but they go on fighting.

TYBALT (*Entering*) Benvolio! What are you doing? Fighting our servants? Turn and fight *me*!

BENVOLIO You're wrong, Tybalt. I don't want to fight anyone. I'm just trying to keep the peace!

TYBALT That's not true! You Montagues are all the same. I'm going to kill you! (*He pulls out his sword and starts fighting with Benvolio. Lord and Lady Capulet enter.*)

LORD CAPULET Look! The Montagues are trying to kill Tybalt! Quickly – bring me a sword!

LADY CAPULET A sword? Don't be stupid, Capulet. You're too old! You haven't used a sword for twenty years.

LORD MONTAGUE *(Entering with Lady Montague)* Look!
The Capulets are making trouble again!

LORD CAPULET What did you say, Montague? Trouble?
The man that started the fight was your nephew
Benvolio! (*He starts to shake Lord Montague.*)

LORD MONTAGUE Let me go, Capulet, you old criminal!

LORD CAPULET Criminal? Old? I'll kill you! (*They begin
fighting. Prince Escalus enters.*)

PRINCE ESCALUS Stop! Montague! Capulet! Stop it
immediately! Tybalt! Benvolio! Stop fighting now,
or I will execute all of you! (*The fighting stops,
and everyone is quiet.*) Listen. I'm very angry.
Verona is a rich, beautiful town, but there is
fighting in the streets nearly every day. Montague,
Capulet, come here. You must tell your families
to stop fighting. Do you understand?

LORD MONTAGUE AND LORD CAPULET Yes, sir.

PRINCE ESCALUS Why is there this argument between your
families? How did it start?

LORD MONTAGUE I can't remember, sir.

LORD CAPULET The argument started a long time ago, sir.

PRINCE ESCALUS The fighting must stop. We must have
peace in Verona.

*Prince Escalus leaves. Then Lord and Lady
Capulet, Tybalt and all the servants leave.*

LORD MONTAGUE The Prince is right, Benvolio.

2

'Stop fighting now, or I will execute all of you!'

BENVOLIO I agree. I was trying to stop the fighting when
Tybalt and the others arrived.

LADY MONTAGUE Have you seen our son, Romeo? He
wasn't in the fight. I'm very happy about that.

BENVOLIO I saw Romeo earlier today. It was about four
o'clock in the morning and still dark. He was
walking, alone, through the woods.

LORD MONTAGUE What's the matter with Romeo? He's
very quiet these days. Sometimes he stays in his
room all day. I think that he's unhappy about
something. Will you try to talk to him, Benvolio?

Romeo enters.

BENVOLIO Look – here he is now. I'll talk to him. *(Lord
and Lady Montague leave.)* What's wrong,
Romeo? What's the matter with you?

ROMEO I'm in love, Benvolio. I'm in love with a beautiful
girl called Rosaline.

BENVOLIO Then why are you unhappy?

ROMEO Because she doesn't love me. She doesn't love
anyone. She says that she's never going to marry.

BENVOLIO There are hundreds of beautiful girls in
Verona. If she doesn't love you, forget about her.

ROMEO I can't do that! Rosaline is the most wonderful
girl in the world. I will never love anyone else.

ACT 1 SCENE 2
Exciting news

A street in Verona. Lord Capulet and Paris are talking.

PARIS Lord Capulet, I have something to tell you. You
already know that I love your daughter Juliet.
Well, I would like to marry her.

LORD CAPULET My daughter is very young, Paris. She's
only thirteen. I don't want her to marry yet. You
must wait for a year or two. Juliet doesn't really
know you.

PARIS   But I love her. If she marries me, she will be very
         happy, I'm sure.

LORD CAPULET   Paris, I'm having a party this evening.
         Juliet will be there, and many other beautiful
         girls will be there too. Come to the party. Enjoy
         yourself. You can talk to Juliet. Perhaps she will
         like you, perhaps not. Remember, she is very
         young. (*A servant enters. Capulet gives the
         servant a piece of paper.*) I want you to go and
         ask a lot of people to my party tonight. Here are
         their names. I would like them all to come.
         Lord Capulet and Paris leave.

SERVANT   But I can't read! What shall I do? I know! I'll
         ask someone to read it for me.
         Romeo and Benvolio enter.
         (*To Romeo*) Excuse me, sir – can you read out
         these names for me? I have to ask all these
         people to come to Lord Capulet's party tonight.
         He gives Romeo the paper.

ROMEO   Martino and his wife and daughters – Valentino
         and his cousins – Tybalt – Lucio – Livia –
         Rosaline – Rosaline! Benvolio, we must go to
         Capulet's party! Rosaline will be there!

BENVOLIO   But Romeo, Capulet and your father are
         enemies!

ROMEO   That doesn't matter. I must see Rosaline!

Lady Capulet's plan

*The Capulets' house. Lady Capulet, Juliet and the
Nurse are talking. Lady Capulet is sitting on a chair.*

LADY CAPULET Tell me, Juliet, how old are you now?

NURSE She's nearly fourteen. Aren't you, my dear?

JULIET That's right. My fourteenth birthday is in two
weeks.

LADY CAPULET Have you thought about marrying, my dear?

NURSE A husband for Juliet! How exciting!

JULIET Marrying? No, I've never thought about it.

LADY CAPULET Well, you must think about it now. A young man wants to marry you. His name is Paris, and

'But I don't know him!'

6

he is young, rich and good-looking. He is a
friend of the Prince of Verona. I want you to try
very, very hard to love him.

JULIET   But I don't know him!

LADY CAPULET   That doesn't matter. You'll meet him this
evening, at the party. You will like him, I'm sure.

NURSE   He'll be a wonderful husband for you, my dear!

ACT 1 SCENE 4
Romeo meets Juliet

The Capulets' house. The party has started, and there is
music, singing and dancing. Lord and Lady Capulet,
Juliet, Tybalt, Paris, the Nurse, servants, musicians and
others are at the party.

LORD CAPULET   Enjoy yourselves, my friends! Everybody is
going to dance tonight. More light! More drinks!
Musicians – play louder! We're going to have a
wonderful party! (*Romeo, Benvolio and*
Mercutio enter. They are wearing masks.)

LADY CAPULET   Who are those men who've just come in? I
can't see their faces, because they are wearing
masks.

LORD CAPULET   I don't know who they are. It doesn't
matter. They look friendly. Give me another

drink! What a wonderful party! Oh, why can't I be young again? Shall we dance?

LADY CAPULET Dance? Don't be stupid, Capulet. You're too old! You haven't danced for twenty years. Come and sit down for a while.

They sit down.

MERCUTIO Don't you want to dance, Romeo?

ROMEO No, I don't, Mercutio. You can dance if you want. I'll wait here.

Benvolio and Mercutio leave, and start dancing.

ROMEO (*He sees Juliet, who is dancing with Paris.*) What a beautiful girl! Who is she? I must meet her! When she stops dancing, I'll go and talk to her.

TYBALT Uncle Capulet! That man is a Montague!

LORD CAPULET Which man?

TYBALT The man who came in a few minutes ago. Over there – the man who's wearing a mask. I know his voice. His name is Romeo, and he's a Montague. I'm going to kill him!

LORD CAPULET No, Tybalt! The Capulets and the Montagues must not fight any more. The Prince of Verona told us to stop fighting. Don't you remember? Romeo is a good man, and you mustn't hurt him. Do you understand?

TYBALT All right, uncle. But I'm very angry. He was wrong to come here. *(He leaves.)*

ROMEO (*To Juliet*) I don't know your name. I saw you just a few minutes ago. I want to talk to you, but I don't know what to say.

JULIET You don't have to say anything.

ROMEO I've never seen anyone as beautiful as you. Can I hold your hand?

JULIET But I don't know you! (*Laughing*) Yes, of course you can hold my hand.

ROMEO (*He holds her hand.*) If our hands can touch, our lips can touch too. (*He kisses her.*)
The Nurse enters.

NURSE Juliet! Where are you? Oh, there you are. Your mother wants you. Come with me, my dear.

ROMEO (*To the Nurse*) Who is her mother?

NURSE Her mother is the lady of the house, and married to Lord Capulet.

ROMEO This is terrible! Lord Capulet is my father's enemy. I love Juliet, but we can never meet again!

'Her mother is married to Lord Capulet.'

9

JULIET   *(Watching Romeo leave)* Nurse, what's that
          young man's name? Over there, the one who's
          leaving. If he has a wife, I'll die unmarried.

NURSE   His name is Romeo, and he's a Montague, the
          only son of your family's great enemy.

JULIET   My only love, a hated Montague!

NURSE   What was that? Come, Juliet. Your mother is
          waiting.

ACT 2 SCENE 1

A secret

*Benvolio, Mercutio and Romeo are in the garden outside
the Capulets' house. Romeo is hiding from the others.*

BENVOLIO   Come on, Mercutio. It's late. Let's go home.
          Where's Romeo?

MERCUTIO   I saw him a few minutes ago. Romeo! Romeo!
          Come on, forget about Rosaline! *(He laughs.)*
          Forget about love! Come with us!
          They leave, then Romeo comes out.

ROMEO   It's easy for him to laugh – he's never been in
          love. I must be near Juliet. I love her.
          Juliet opens a window and looks out.
          But look! What light is that? It is the east, and
          Juliet is the sun! *(He hides.)*

'Call me love, not Romeo.'

JULIET   Oh, Romeo! What's in a name? You are a Montague and I am a Capulet. They're just names, they don't mean anything. Why are our families enemies? I love you, and that's the only thing that matters.

ROMEO   You're right, Juliet. (*He comes out again.*) Nothing else is important. Call me love, not Romeo.

JULIET   I know that voice. Romeo! Why did you come here? If my cousin finds you here, he'll kill you.

ROMEO   It's love that brings me here. I am not afraid of Capulet swords. I think nothing of the danger, if you really love me.

JULIET   Romeo – you've already heard me say it – I love

11

you. Do you love me? Perhaps I love you too much. Perhaps it's wrong to say so openly that I love you . . .

ROMEO Lady, I love you and I will always love you. Tell me, when can we be together – together for the rest of our lives?

The Nurse calls out from inside the house.

JULIET Oh, Romeo – I must go. Listen. If you really want to marry me, I'll send my Nurse to you tomorrow. Give her a message for me. Tell me when and where to meet you, and I'll follow you, my lord, anywhere in the world. Good night, my love.

ROMEO Good night, sweet Juliet. (*Juliet closes the window and goes inside.*) I must talk to the priest, Father Lawrence. I'll ask him to marry us, secretly, without telling our families.

ACT 2 SCENE 2
Help from Father Lawrence

It is early in the morning. Father Lawrence is in his garden.

FATHER LAWRENCE I use these flowers to make medicines. The medicines are good, but they can be dangerous. So I make them very, very carefully.

Romeo enters.

Good morning, Romeo. It's very early. What's the matter – can't you sleep?

ROMEO No, I can't, Father Lawrence. I'm in love, and I need your help.

FATHER LAWRENCE You're in love with Rosaline, aren't you?

ROMEO Rosaline? No, Father, I never think about her now. I'm in love with Juliet, Lord Capulet's daughter.

FATHER LAWRENCE This is very sudden! Does she love you?

ROMEO Yes, she does. We want to marry, and we want to do it today. But we must do it secretly. If we tell our families, they'll stop us. You'll help us, won't you?

FATHER LAWRENCE I'm not sure. Your families are enemies, aren't they?

ROMEO Yes, Father. But that's not important to me, or to Juliet.

FATHER LAWRENCE Wait a minute – if you two marry, perhaps the arguments will finish, and your families will be friends! Yes, Romeo, I'll help you. Come to my house with Juliet this afternoon, and I'll marry you.

ROMEO That's wonderful! Thank you, Father!

ACT 2 SCENE 3
A message for Juliet

A street in Verona. Mercutio and Benvolio are talking.

BENVOLIO Mercutio – have you seen Romeo this morning?

MERCUTIO No. He's not interested in his friends any more. He's only interested in love.

BENVOLIO Tybalt saw Romeo at the party last night, and he's really angry.

MERCUTIO Ha! Who's afraid of Tybalt? Look, here comes Romeo now!

Romeo enters.

BENVOLIO Romeo – where have you been? Don't you want to see your friends any more?

MERCUTIO You're in love with Rosaline, aren't you? That's why you don't want to be with us!

ROMEO (*Laughing*) No, I'm not in love with Rosaline.

BENVOLIO Tybalt is angry with you. He saw you at the party.

ROMEO (*Laughing again*) But Tybalt is a Capulet. The Capulets are my friends.

MERCUTIO AND BENVOLIO Your friends! What do you mean?

NURSE (*Entering*) Excuse me. I'm looking for Romeo, Lord Montague's son. Do you know him?

'Romeo's only interested in love.'

MERCUTIO This is Romeo.

NURSE Oh! Isn't he good-looking! I'd like to talk to you,
Romeo. (*She looks at the others.*) Alone, please.
Benvolio and Mercutio leave, laughing.
Juliet asked me to find you. She loves you very
much, you know.

ROMEO And I love her too. I've already spoken to Father
Lawrence, the priest. Tell Juliet to come to his
house this afternoon. He has agreed to marry us.
You mustn't tell her mother or father.

NURSE Don't worry, my dear, I won't tell them. They
want her to marry Paris, but she doesn't like
him! And he's not as good-looking as you!

ROMEO Don't forget to tell her – this afternoon, at
Father Lawrence's house!

ACT 2 SCENE 4
A secret wedding

Father Lawrence's house. Father Lawrence and Romeo are talking.

ROMEO Juliet will be here very soon. I'll be very happy when we're married.

FATHER LAWRENCE Listen, Romeo. You only loved Rosaline for a few weeks. Remember, if you marry Juliet, you must love her, and stay with her, for the rest of your life.

ROMEO Yes, Father, I understand. I'll always love her. *Juliet enters, and kisses Romeo.*

JULIET The Nurse told me to meet you here. She said that Father Lawrence would marry us.

FATHER LAWRENCE And I will. Come with me.

'You only loved Rosaline for a few weeks.'

16

Act 3 Scene 1
More trouble

A busy street in Verona. Some people are walking along the street. Mercutio and Benvolio are talking.

BENVOLIO It's hot today, isn't it? I don't like this weather. People feel angry when it's so hot.
Tybalt and some friends enter.

MERCUTIO Look! It's the Capulets – over there!

BENVOLIO Don't start an argument, Mercutio! We don't want trouble.

MERCUTIO I'm not afraid of Tybalt.

TYBALT Where is Romeo? He's your friend, isn't he?

MERCUTIO That's none of your business.

TYBALT I'm looking for him. And I'm going to find him.

MERCUTIO Are you looking for a fight?

BENVOLIO Stop it, you two! (*Romeo enters.*)

TYBALT There he is! Romeo! Come here! (*He pulls out his sword.*) You came to our house last night, didn't you? Well, we don't want the Montagues in our house. I'm going to teach you a lesson. Come on, get out your sword and fight!

ROMEO Tybalt, I'm not your enemy! (*Laughing*) The Montagues and Capulets are going to be good friends. Something wonderful has happened.

17

TYBALT   What are you talking about?

MERCUTIO   Why won't you fight with him, Romeo? (*He
pulls out his sword.*) Well, I'll fight. Come on!
Mercutio and Tybalt start fighting.

ROMEO   Stop fighting! Don't you remember what Prince
Escalus said? Benvolio, help me to stop them.
*Benvolio and Romeo try to stop them. Tybalt
stabs Mercutio and runs away. Mercutio falls.*

MERCUTIO   Why did you stand between us? I – I'm hurt!

ROMEO   I'm sorry, Mercutio – I was trying to help.

MERCUTIO   I need a doctor. Oh, you Montagues and
Capulets, what a stupid argument! You're both
wrong, to fight, and hate, and fight again like
this! Ah – I'm dying! (*Mercutio dies.*)

'Ah – I'm dying!'

18

'Now I'm going to kill you!'

ROMEO Mercutio! He's dead! Tybalt! Come back! (*He pulls out his sword angrily.*) You've killed my friend. Now I'm going to kill you!
Tybalt enters again. They fight, and Romeo kills him. Some people who are watching start shouting.

BENVOLIO This is terrible! Romeo, run away! You'll be in trouble if the Prince finds you here!

ROMEO Oh, no! What have I done? (*He runs away.*)
Prince Escalus, Lord and Lady Montague, Lord and Lady Capulet, servants and others enter.

PRINCE ESCALUS What's happened? How did these men die?

BENVOLIO Tybalt killed Mercutio, sir. Mercutio was Romeo's friend. Romeo was very angry, and he killed Tybalt.

LADY CAPULET Romeo must die! He's a murderer! He killed my nephew Tybalt!

PRINCE ESCALUS But Tybalt was a murderer too, Lady
Capulet.

LADY CAPULET No, he wasn't! That's what Benvolio says,
but he's a Montague. Romeo must die!

LORD MONTAGUE Sir, our son is not a murderer. He killed
Tybalt because he was angry.

PRINCE ESCALUS Listen, all of you. I have decided not to
execute Romeo. But he must leave Verona, and he
can never come back. Tell him that he must leave
immediately. If he ever comes back to Verona, he
will die. Now go home, and keep the peace.

ACT 3 SCENE 2
Another message

Juliet is alone in her room.

JULIET I'm so excited! Romeo is going to be with me
tonight! We're married now, but the only people
who know are Father Lawrence and my Nurse.
Here she is now. (*The Nurse enters.*)

NURSE Juliet, my dear, something terrible has happened.
(*She starts crying.*) He's dead, he's dead.

JULIET Who's dead? Not Romeo? Not my husband?

NURSE No. Tybalt is dead.

JULIET Oh, no! My cousin Tybalt! How did he die?

NURSE   There was a fight, and Romeo killed him.

JULIET   It can't be true! Romeo never fights.

NURSE   But it *is* true. Tybalt killed Romeo's friend
Mercutio, and Romeo was very angry. The two of
them started fighting, and Romeo killed Tybalt.

JULIET   Where's Romeo now? And what's going to
happen to him?

NURSE   Romeo's hiding in Father Lawrence's house. The
Prince has told Lord Montague that Romeo must
leave Verona and never come back.

JULIET   So I'll never see him again! (*She starts crying.*)

NURSE   Don't cry, my dear. Listen. I'll go to Father
Lawrence's house and tell Romeo to come here
secretly tonight, to say goodbye to you.

JULIET   Thank you, Nurse. You're very kind. Wait –
take this ring. (*She gives her a ring.*) Give it to
Romeo, and tell him that I love him.

ACT 3 SCENE 3
Bad news for Romeo

*Father Lawrence's house. Romeo is hiding. Father
Lawrence enters.*

FATHER LAWRENCE   Romeo – where are you? It's me, Father
Lawrence. (*Romeo comes out.*)

ROMEO What did Prince Escalus say? Am I going to die?

FATHER LAWRENCE No. Killing Tybalt was wrong, but the Prince is not going to execute you. He said that you must leave Verona immediately, and never come back.

ROMEO This is terrible! (*He starts crying.*) Leaving Juliet is worse than dying.

FATHER LAWRENCE Just listen, Romeo. You are lucky. The Prince has been kind to you.

ROMEO But I want to die! I can't live without Juliet! *There is a knock on the door.*

FATHER LAWRENCE Hide, Romeo! If anyone finds you here, there will be trouble!

ROMEO It doesn't matter. I want to die. *The Nurse enters.*

FATHER LAWRENCE I'm happy to see you, Nurse. Have you been with Juliet?

NURSE Yes. I saw her a few minutes ago, crying and shaking, just like Romeo here.

ROMEO But I killed her cousin. Does she still love me?

NURSE Yes, of course she does. (*She gives Romeo Juliet's ring.*) She sends you this ring.

FATHER LAWRENCE Listen, Romeo. You can go to see Juliet tonight. But then you must leave Verona. Later, I will tell everybody that you and Juliet are married, and I will ask the Prince to think again.

Perhaps you can come back to Verona soon. But
you have to leave Verona tonight and go to
Mantua. Do you agree to do that?

ROMEO   Yes, Father. How long must I stay in Mantua?

FATHER LAWRENCE   I'm not sure. Stay there until I send you
a message. Don't come back until you hear from
me. Now go and say goodbye to Juliet.

ACT 3 SCENE 4
Lord Capulet's plan

*The Capulets' house. Lord and Lady Capulet and Paris
are talking.*

LORD CAPULET   Paris, my daughter is very unhappy. Her
cousin Tybalt died this morning. Lord
Montague's son killed him.

PARIS   I'm sorry to hear that. Can I talk to Juliet?

LADY CAPULET   Not at the moment, Paris. She is in her
room. It's very late, and she needs to rest.

LORD CAPULET   Listen. I've just thought of something. I
want Juliet to forget about Tybalt's death. I
think that she'll be happy when she marries. I
know that you love Juliet, and that you would
like to marry her. The two of you must marry as
soon as possible. What day is it today?

PARIS   It's Monday night, sir.

LORD CAPULET   Right. The wedding will be on Thursday.

PARIS   That's wonderful!

LORD CAPULET   (*To his wife*) Go and tell Juliet what I have
decided, my dear. We must hurry! Don't forget,
Paris – the wedding will be in three days!

PARIS   I won't forget, sir!

ACT 3 SCENE 5

Trouble for Juliet

Juliet's room. Romeo and Juliet are together.

ROMEO   I'm sorry, my love, but I have to go. Look
outside – it's nearly morning.

JULIET   Please don't say that. I want you to stay with me.
You are my husband now. You needn't go.

ROMEO   You know that I have to go. If anyone finds me
here, the Prince will execute me. I'm going to
stay in Mantua. Father Lawrence is going to talk
to our families, and to the Prince. Then he will
send me a message. Perhaps I'll be back soon.

JULIET   I hope so, Romeo, my only love!
There is a knock at the door.

ROMEO   Kiss me! Goodbye, my love.
He climbs out of the window.

LADY CAPULET (*Entering*) Juliet – you're already out of bed. It's very early.

JULIET I know. I can't sleep.

LADY CAPULET You're still very unhappy about your cousin Tybalt. Don't worry, my dear. We'll find Romeo. And when we find him, he'll die. Now listen, I have some exciting news. Your father has said that Paris and you can marry. And the wedding will be on Thursday. (*Juliet screams.*)

JULIET I won't marry Paris. It's just not possible!

LADY CAPULET What do you mean?

Lord Capulet and the Nurse enter.

LORD CAPULET Have you told her the news?

LADY CAPULET She says that she won't marry Paris.

LORD CAPULET What? Why not? Listen, Juliet. Paris is a good, kind man. He's an important man, too, and a friend of the Prince's. You are a very lucky girl!

'You are a very lucky girl!'

25

JULIET   Father, listen. I know that you're trying to help me, but I will never marry Paris. I don't love him. I don't even know him.

LORD CAPULET   That doesn't matter. You will marry him on Thursday. Do you understand?
Lord and Lady Capulet leave.

JULIET   This is terrible. What shall I do? They don't know that I've married Romeo!

NURSE   Listen, my dear. Romeo is in Mantua. Perhaps you'll never see him again. Your mother and father are right, you know. Paris is a kind man, and good-looking too. He'll be a better husband than Romeo. Marry him. Forget about Romeo. That's the best thing to do. *(She leaves.)*

JULIET   I will never listen to my Nurse again. I thought that she would help me, but she won't. I'm going to see Father Lawrence. Perhaps *he* can help me.

ACT 4 SCENE 1
Father Lawrence's medicine

Father Lawrence's house. Paris and Father Lawrence are talking.

FATHER LAWRENCE   What! On Thursday! That's in two days. This is very sudden!

PARIS   I know. I'm very excited. I've loved Juliet for a long time, and soon we'll be married!

FATHER LAWRENCE   But you don't know her very well. You must wait, Paris. Thursday is too soon.

PARIS   But her father has already decided. I'm very happy!

JULIET   (*Entering*) Good morning, Paris.

PARIS   Hello, Juliet, my love. (*Laughing*) You'll soon be my wife.

JULIET   Perhaps. I've come to talk to the priest.

PARIS   Are you going to tell him how much you love me?

JULIET   I've come to talk to him alone.

FATHER LAWRENCE   Can you leave us, please, Paris?

PARIS   Of course, Father. Goodbye, my love. (*He kisses Juliet.*) We'll be married soon! (*He leaves.*)

JULIET   What shall I do? (*She starts crying.*) I want to die.

FATHER LAWRENCE   You must marry Paris. What else can you do?

JULIET   Father, I'll never marry Paris. Don't you understand? I love Romeo. He is my husband. Look, I have a knife. (*She pulls out a knife.*) If you tell me to marry Paris, I'll kill myself.

FATHER LAWRENCE   Stop! Put down the knife. Listen, Juliet, I've just thought of something. (*He goes to a cupboard and takes out a bottle.*)

JULIET   What's that? Is it poison? Will it kill me?

27

FATHER LAWRENCE No, Juliet, it's not poison, but it's a very, very strong medicine. Anyone who drinks this will sleep for two days.

JULIET What do you want me to do?

FATHER LAWRENCE I want you to drink this medicine the night before your wedding. You'll sleep very, very deeply, and it won't be possible to wake you up. You will be cold and still. Everyone will think that you are dead.

JULIET What'll happen then?

FATHER LAWRENCE They'll put your body in your family's tomb, next to your cousin Tybalt. Later, you'll wake up. (*Juliet screams.*) Don't worry, I'll send a message to Romeo in Mantua, and tell him to come back to Verona when it's dark. I'll tell him to go to the tomb and open it at night. Then the two of you can run away together to Mantua. Will you do it? It's very dangerous, but if you don't do this, you'll have to marry Paris.

JULIET Yes, Father, I'll do it. I'll do anything to be with Romeo. Thank you, Father.
Juliet takes the bottle and leaves.

FATHER LAWRENCE Father John! Father John! (*Father John enters. Father Lawrence quickly writes a message and gives it to him.*) Take this message to Romeo in Mantua. It's very, very important.

ACT 4 SCENE 2
Another wedding

The Capulets' house. Lord and Lady Capulet, the Nurse and servants are all busy.

LORD CAPULET *(To a servant)* Go and ask all our friends to
come to the wedding. *(To another servant)* Go
and find the best cooks in Verona. This will be a
very special wedding. *(To the Nurse)* Where's
Juliet?

NURSE She's with the priest, sir. She'll be back soon.
Look, here she is now. She looks very happy.

JULIET *(Entering)* I'm sorry, father.

LORD CAPULET What?

JULIET You told me to marry Paris, and you were right.
I'm not going to cry any more. He is the right
man for me. I'm sorry that I didn't agree at first.

LORD CAPULET This is wonderful news! Oh, I'm so happy!
Listen, everybody! The wedding will be
tomorrow morning. Go and tell Paris.

LADY CAPULET Tomorrow? But tomorrow's Wednesday.
You said that the wedding would be on
Thursday. We won't be ready tomorrow!

LORD CAPULET That doesn't matter. Juliet and Paris must
marry as soon as possible. Hurry, hurry!

29

Nobody will sleep tonight – we're all going to be too busy. Nurse – go and help Juliet with her wedding-dress! Oh, I'm so happy!

Juliet drinks the medicine

Juliet's room. Juliet is wearing her wedding-dress. The nurse and Lady Capulet are with her.

NURSE You look beautiful, my dear.

LADY CAPULET You must go to bed now, Juliet. It's very late, and you need to rest. Good night.
The Nurse and Lady Capulet leave.

JULIET They think that I'm going to marry Paris tomorrow, but they're wrong. (*She takes out*

'They'll think I'm dead.'

30

Father Lawrence's bottle.) When I drink this, I'll fall asleep. They'll think I'm dead. Oh, I'm so afraid! I won't wake up for two days. When I wake up, I'll be in the tomb, with dead bodies around me. But I must do it. Romeo will come and find me, and we'll be together again!
She drinks the medicine and lies down on her bed.

Act 4 Scene 4
The Capulets find Juliet

The Capulets' house. It is early in the morning, and Lord and Lady Capulet, the Nurse, servants and cooks are all moving around busily.

LADY CAPULET We need more food! And more tables and chairs!

LORD CAPULET Bring those flowers over here! Hurry up, there isn't much time left!

NURSE Why don't you go to bed, sir? It's very late.

LORD CAPULET I can't sleep – I'm too excited! My daughter is going to marry Paris in the morning! After the wedding, we're going to have a party. It'll be the best party I've ever had!

LADY CAPULET Paris will be here soon. Nurse – go and wake Juliet up.

31

The Nurse goes out.

LORD CAPULET I can hear music. Paris is coming, with his
musicians. (*The musicians play outside.*)

NURSE Help! Help! *(Some servants run to help her.)*

LADY CAPULET What's the matter?

*The Nurse and servants come back, carrying
Juliet. They are crying unhappily.*

NURSE She's dead!

Everyone stops moving.

LADY CAPULET Juliet! My only child! (*Holding Juliet*)
Please, wake up! Oh, she's cold! She's dead!

LORD CAPULET She was the sweetest child in the world.
She was only thirteen, and now she's dead.
*Father Lawrence, Paris and the musicians enter.
The musicians are still playing.*

PARIS I've come to take Juliet to church!
*They see Juliet's body. The musicians stop
playing.*

LADY CAPULET She was our only child. Now our lives are
empty. We will never be happy again.

PARIS Juliet – dead? This is the worst day of my life.

FATHER LAWRENCE Carry her to the church. We will put
her in your family's tomb, next to her cousin.
Put flowers on her body.
They put flowers on her body and carry her out.

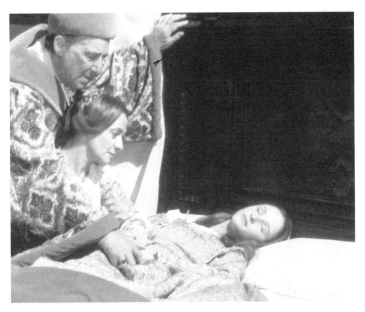

'She was the sweetest child in the world.'

News from Verona

Romeo is walking along a street in Mantua. There are some shops in the street.

ROMEO Oh, I'm so lonely without Juliet! I want to go back to Verona, but I can't go back yet. I must wait until Father Lawrence sends a message. I'll hear some news soon, I hope. (*One of Lord Montague's servants enters.*) Did Father Lawrence send you?

SERVANT No, but I've got some news. It's bad news, I'm
afraid. Juliet is dead. I saw them put her body in
the Capulets' tomb yesterday.

ROMEO What! I must go back. I must find out what's
happened.

SERVANT Wait, my lord. Don't go back yet. Wait until
Father Lawrence sends some news.

ROMEO (*Shouting angrily*) No! I'm going to Verona now.
Leave me alone. (*The servant leaves.*) If Juliet is
dead, I want to die too. I'm going to see Juliet
once more, and then I'm going to die. I need
some poison. Where can I find some poison? I
remember seeing a shop near here. Where was it?
Here it is. (*He stops outside a shop.*) You! You
sell medicines, don't you?

SHOPKEEPER Yes, sir.

ROMEO I want some poison. It must be strong. Do you
understand?

SHOPKEEPER Sir, I sell medicines to help people, not
poison to kill them.

ROMEO Here. (*He takes some gold from his pocket.*) I
will give you as much gold as you want. You
look poor and hungry.

SHOPKEEPER Yes, sir, I am. (*He goes to a cupboard and
takes out a bottle.*) I have some poison. It is very
dangerous. Anyone who drinks this will die

immediately. But I can't sell it to you, sir. It's a
crime. If I sell this poison to you, I'll be in trouble.

ROMEO Don't worry. I won't tell anyone that it came
from your shop. (*He takes some more gold from
his pocket.*) Here, have all my gold. I don't need
it. (*The shopkeeper gives him the bottle, and
Romeo leaves.*)

FATHER JOHN (*Entering*) Where's Romeo? I've got a
message for him. It's from Father Lawrence. He
said that the message was very important.
(*Running up and down the street*) Romeo! Romeo!
Where are you? Romeo! Oh, no! He's not here!

ACT 5 SCENE 2
Together again

*A garden outside a church. It is late at night. Paris is
standing near the Capulets' tomb. It is a very large tomb
with a big, heavy door.*

PARIS Oh, Juliet! I loved you more than anyone else in
the world. I wanted you to be my wife, but now
you're dead. (*Putting flowers on the tomb*) I'm
going to come to your tomb every night. What's
that noise? Someone's coming!
He hides, and Romeo enters.

ROMEO   Juliet – I must see your sweet face again!
        Paris comes out. Romeo opens the door of the tomb.

PARIS   Stop! You're Romeo, aren't you? You're one of the Montagues. What are you doing to Juliet's tomb?

ROMEO   Who are you? Leave me alone! (*The two men fight, and Romeo kills Paris. Romeo goes into the tomb, and takes the bottle of poison out of his pocket.*) Juliet, my love, my wife! You are dead, but you are still beautiful. This will be our last kiss. (*He kisses her, then drinks the poison.*) So, with a kiss, I die. (*He dies.*)

FATHER LAWRENCE (*Entering*) Juliet will wake up very soon. Where's Romeo? Father John took a message to him, and the message told him to meet me here. Romeo! (*He goes to the tomb.*) The door's open! What's happened?

JULIET (*Waking up*) Father Lawrence! It's good to see you. Where's Romeo?

FATHER LAWRENCE Juliet – something terrible has happened. Romeo is lying next to you, but he's dead! Quickly – get out of the tomb, and come with me. If anyone finds us here, there will be trouble!

JULIET No, Father, I want to be with Romeo. (*Father Lawrence runs away.*) Romeo, my love, what's happened? (*She sees the bottle of poison.*) He's

36

killed himself! Well, I'm going to die too. I can't live without him. Romeo, perhaps there's poison on your lips. If I kiss you, perhaps I will die too. (*She kisses him.*) I'm still alive, but I want to die. I'm not afraid of death. (*She takes out a knife, stabs herself and dies. Some people enter.*)

PEOPLE (*Shouting*) What's happening? Look, here's Paris – he's dead! And Romeo's dead, too! Someone's opened the tomb! Find the Prince! Find the Capulets and the Montagues! (*Prince Escalus, the Capulets, Montagues and servants enter.*)

PRINCE ESCALUS Dead? Romeo and Juliet? (*Some more*

'They have both killed themselves.'

people enter, with Father Lawrence.) Father
Lawrence, do you know anything about this?

FATHER LAWRENCE Just a few days ago, Romeo married
Juliet. (*Everyone shouts in surprise, and Lady
Capulet starts crying.*) I married them secretly,
because the Capulets and Montagues are enemies.
Juliet didn't want to marry Paris, so I told her to
take some special medicine. She wasn't dead, she
was asleep. I wanted to send a message to Romeo
in Mantua, but he didn't get the message. And
now they have both killed themselves.

PRINCE ESCALUS Lord Capulet, Lord Montague – come here.
(*They stand in front of the Prince.*) This has
happened because you are enemies. Romeo,
Juliet, Paris, Mercutio and Tybalt are all dead.

LORD CAPULET Sir, our arguments have finished. We are
friends now, and we will never fight again.
They shake hands unhappily.

LORD MONTAGUE We'll build a statue of Romeo and Juliet.
It will be made of gold. No one will ever forget
them.

PRINCE ESCALUS Perhaps Verona will be peaceful now. (*He
looks up at the sky.*) There's no sun this morning.
Go home now, all of you, and remember this
unhappy story of Juliet and her Romeo.

GLOSSARY

argument angry shouting that sometimes happens when people don't agree

cousin your uncle's or aunt's child

else different, other

enter to come in

execute to punish someone (for a crime) by killing him or her

good-looking beautiful, handsome

hate opposite of 'to love'

kiss to touch someone with the lips in a loving way

lady a title for a woman of good family

lips the front parts of the mouth

lord a title for a man of good family

mask a cover that you put over the face to hide it

medicine a special drink that helps someone who is ill to get better

message some news or information that you want to write to or tell someone

musician someone who plays a musical instrument

nephew your brother's or sister's son

peace when people live quietly, with no fighting or arguments

poison something that will kill you or make you very ill if you eat or drink it

priest a person who works for the church, a church leader

prince the son of a king or queen

servant someone who works (for example, cooking or cleaning) in another person's house

shopkeeper someone who has a small shop

sir a polite way to speak to a man who is more important than you

stab to hurt someone with a knife or sword

statue a figure of a person, (in this story) made of gold

sword a very long, sharp kind of knife used for fighting

tomb (in this story) a large stone room, often in or near a church, where dead bodies from the same family are kept or buried

uncle your mother's or father's brother

wedding when a man and woman marry (often in a church)

Romeo and Juliet

ACTIVITIES

ACTIVITIES

Before Reading

1 **The play is set in Verona, northern Italy, in the fifteenth century. How do you think life was different then? Tick one box for each sentence.**

	YES	NO
1 Girls often married very young.	☐	☐
2 Girls could choose their husbands.	☐	☐
3 Men often carried swords.	☐	☐
4 Everyone could read and write.	☐	☐
5 There were police in the cities.	☐	☐

2 **Read the information on the first page of the book, and the back cover. Are these sentences true (T) or false (F)? Change the false sentences into true ones.**

1 Romeo is a Montague.
2 The Montagues and Capulets like each other.
3 Romeo and Juliet fall in love.
4 Juliet wants to marry Paris.
5 Lord Capulet is Juliet's father.
6 Paris is a friend of Romeo's.
7 Juliet has to leave Verona.

3 Can you guess who will say these things in the play? Match the words with the people.

'The Capulets are making trouble again!'

'My fourteenth birthday is in two weeks.'

'Lord Capulet, you already know that I love your daughter Juliet.'

'What a beautiful girl! Who is she? I must meet her!'

'She says that she won't marry Paris.'

'Listen, my dear. Your mother and father are right, you know.'

Juliet

Juliet's Nurse

Lord Montague

Lady Capulet

Romeo

Paris

4 Before you read Act 1 Scenes 1 and 2, can you guess what's going to happen? These are the scene titles:

Scene 1: *Trouble in Verona*
Scene 2: *Exciting news*

1 Why is there trouble in Verona?
   a) Romeo is in love with Juliet.
   b) The Montagues and Capulets are fighting.
   c) The Prince of Verona has died.

2 What is the exciting news?
   a) The Capulets are having a party.
   b) Romeo and Juliet are going to marry.
   c) The two families agree to be friends.

43

While Reading

Read Act 1, then answer these questions.

1 Who tries to stop the servants fighting?
2 Why can't Lord Capulet fight?
3 Why is Lord Montague worried about his son?
4 Why does Romeo want to go to the Capulets' party?
5 At Lord Capulet's party, who wants to kill Romeo?

Read Act 2. Who said these words in this act?

1 'Forget about love! Come with us!'
2 'What's in a name?'
3 'I am not afraid of Capulet swords.'
4 'The medicines are good, but they can be dangerous.'
5 'Oh! Isn't he good-looking!'

Before you read Act 3, can you guess what's going to happen? There's going to be some fighting. What are these people going to do?

Tybalt   Mercutio   Benvolio
Romeo   Prince Escalus

Read Act 3. Are these sentences true (T) or false (F)?

1 Romeo and Juliet have married secretly.
2 Benvolio starts a fight with Tybalt.
3 Romeo kills Tybalt.
4 Prince Escalus decides to execute Romeo.
5 Juliet's parents want her to marry Paris.

Read Act 4. Here are some untrue sentences about this act. Change them into true sentences.

1 Juliet wants to marry Paris.
2 Father Lawrence gives Juliet some strong poison.
3 Father Lawrence gives Father John an important message for Paris.
4 Lord Capulet wants Juliet and Paris to marry next month.
5 After Juliet drinks the medicine, she dies.
6 The Capulets put Juliet in the family's tomb, next to Mercutio.

Read Act 5. Who said this – Paris or Romeo?

1 'If Juliet is dead, I want to die too.'
2 'I wanted you to be my wife, but now you're dead.'
3 'I'm going to come to your tomb every night.'
4 'So, with a kiss, I die.'

After Reading

1 **Match these parts of sentences, and put them in the correct order to make a summary of the story.**

1 The Capulets thought Juliet was dead, and

2 Romeo killed Tybalt in an argument, and

3 Father Lawrence gave Juliet some medicine, and

4 When Juliet woke up, she killed herself because

5 When Romeo found Juliet in the tomb,

6 Romeo and Juliet fell in love, but

7 Lord Capulet told Juliet that

8 . . . their families were enemies.

9 . . . he had to leave Verona.

10 . . . she didn't want to live without Romeo.

11 . . . she had to marry Paris.

12 . . . she slept for two days.

13 . . . he drank some poison and died.

14 . . . they put her body in the family's tomb.

2 **Father Lawrence wrote a message and told Father John to take it to Romeo. What did it say? Complete the message with words from this list.**

asleep, back, important, medicine, meet, midnight, parents, together, tomb, wakes, worry

Romeo – this message is _____! You must come _____ to Verona. _____ me outside the Capulets' _____ at _____. Juliet will be in there. But don't _____ – she's not dead! I've given her some strong _____, and she will be _____. When she _____ up, you can run away _____ to Mantua. Her _____ wanted her to marry Paris, but she wants to be with you.

3 **Find the answers to this crossword in the play.**

1 When things are quiet and there is no fighting. (5)

2 If you wear this, people can't see your face. (4)

3 Don't eat or drink this – it can kill you! (6)

4 A pianist, violinist or guitarist, for example. (8)

5 Your mother's or father's brother. (5)

6 This sometimes happens when people don't agree. (8)

7 To hurt someone with a knife. (4)

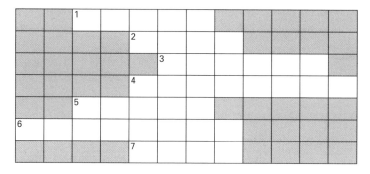

What is the hidden word in the crossword? It is the name of a family. Write three things you know about people in this family.

4 What did you think about the people in the play? Choose some names, and complete some of these sentences.

Lord Montague / Romeo / Father Lawrence / the Nurse / Tybalt / Lady Capulet / Mercutio / Benvolio / Juliet

1 I felt sorry for _____ because _____ .
2 I felt angry at _____ because _____ .
3 _____ was right to _____ .
4 _____ was wrong to _____ .
5 I think _____ did a bad thing when _____ .
6 I think _____ did a good thing when _____ .
7 I think _____ was a nice person but _____ .

5 Father John is in Mantua, looking for Romeo. He is talking to the shopkeeper. Put their conversation in the correct order and write in their names. Father John speaks first (number 6).

1 _____ 'Yes, I did. I didn't want to. But he was angry. What could I do?'
2 _____ 'What did he say?'
3 _____ 'He wanted some very strong medicine. I tried to say no, but–'
4 _____ 'But you know very well that's a crime! Did he give you a lot of money?'
5 _____ 'How did he look? Was he happy or sad?'
6 _____ 'I'm looking for a young man called Montague. I have an important message for him. Have you seen him?'

7 _____ 'He didn't say very much. He wanted – some
  medicine.'

8 _____ 'He gave me some gold. He said that he didn't
  need it. He saw that I am poor and hungry, and he
  wanted to help me.'

9 _____ 'He looked sad and angry. He was in a hurry.'

10 _____ 'A young man came into my shop about half an
  hour ago. I didn't ask his name.'

11 _____ 'This is terrible! I must find him. Perhaps he's
  going to kill someone – or himself!'

12 _____ 'Medicine? What kind of medicine?'

13 _____ 'Now, tell me the truth. Did you sell him poison?'

Was the shopkeeper wrong to sell poison to Romeo? Why?

6 **Here are some other titles for the play. Which are good
and which are not good? Can you explain why?**

A Secret Love   *Death in Verona*   *Friends and Enemies*
  Peace at last   *Too Young to Die*   *Together in Death*

7 **Do you agree or disagree with these sentences? Explain
why.**

1 You must never keep a secret from your parents.

2 You must fight people who say bad things about you.

3 Parents must always help their children to choose a
  husband or wife.

4 Love is more important than money.

49

ABOUT THE AUTHOR

William Shakespeare (1564–1616) was born in Stratford-upon-Avon, a small town in central England. He went to school in Stratford, and he married when he was only eighteen years old. A few years later, he moved to London, while his wife and children stayed in Stratford. He worked as an actor, and soon started writing plays and poetry. At that time, theatres were new and exciting places. There were only a few theatres in England, and they were all in London.

When Shakespeare was only thirty, he wrote *Romeo and Juliet*. It was an immediate success. Most plays then were about kings and queens, but thousands of people came to see this sad story of two young lovers. For the next fifteen years, Shakespeare lived in London, although he bought a large house in Stratford for his family. He wrote more than thirty plays, and Queen Elizabeth I often saw his plays.

When he was in his late forties, Shakespeare returned to Stratford for a quiet life with his family away from the theatre. He died in 1616, when he was only fifty-two years old.

OXFORD BOOKWORMS LIBRARY

Classics • Crime & Mystery • Factfiles • Fantasy & Horror
Human Interest • Playscripts • Thriller & Adventure
True Stories • World Stories

The OXFORD BOOKWORMS LIBRARY provides enjoyable reading in English, with a wide range of classic and modern fiction, non-fiction, and plays. It includes original and adapted texts in seven carefully graded language stages, which take learners from beginner to advanced level. An overview is given on the next pages.

All Stage 1 titles are available as audio recordings, as well as over eighty other titles from Starter to Stage 6. All Starters and many titles at Stages 1 to 4 are specially recommended for younger learners. Every Bookworm is illustrated, and Starters and Factfiles have full-colour illustrations.

The OXFORD BOOKWORMS LIBRARY also offers extensive support. Each book contains an introduction to the story, notes about the author, a glossary, and activities. Additional resources include tests and worksheets, and answers for these and for the activities in the books. There is advice on running a class library, using audio recordings, and the many ways of using Oxford Bookworms in reading programmes. Resource materials are available on the website <www.oup.com/bookworms>.

The *Oxford Bookworms Collection* is a series for advanced learners. It consists of volumes of short stories by well-known authors, both classic and modern. Texts are not abridged or adapted in any way, but carefully selected to be accessible to the advanced student.

You can find details and a full list of titles in the *Oxford Bookworms Library Catalogue* and *Oxford English Language Teaching Catalogues*, and on the website <www.oup.com/bookworms>.

THE OXFORD BOOKWORMS LIBRARY
GRADING AND SAMPLE EXTRACTS

STARTER • 250 HEADWORDS
present simple – present continuous – imperative –
can/cannot, must – *going to* (future) – simple gerunds …

Her phone is ringing – but where is it?

Sally gets out of bed and looks in her bag. No phone. She looks under the bed. No phone. Then she looks behind the door. There is her phone. Sally picks up her phone and answers it. *Sally's Phone*

STAGE 1 • 400 HEADWORDS
… past simple – coordination with *and*, *but*, *or* –
subordination with *before*, *after*, *when*, *because*, *so* …

I knew him in Persia. He was a famous builder and I worked with him there. For a time I was his friend, but not for long. When he came to Paris, I came after him – I wanted to watch him. He was a very clever, very dangerous man. *The Phantom of the Opera*

STAGE 2 • 700 HEADWORDS
… present perfect – *will* (future) – *(don't) have to, must not, could* –
comparison of adjectives – simple *if* clauses – past continuous –
tag questions – *ask/tell* + infinitive …

While I was writing these words in my diary, I decided what to do. I must try to escape. I shall try to get down the wall outside. The window is high above the ground, but I have to try. I shall take some of the gold with me – if I escape, perhaps it will be helpful later. *Dracula*

… should, may – present perfect continuous – *used to* – past perfect –
causative – relative clauses – indirect statements …

Of course, it was most important that no one should see
Colin, Mary, or Dickon entering the secret garden. So Colin
gave orders to the gardeners that they must all keep away
from that part of the garden in future. ***The Secret Garden***

… past perfect continuous – passive (simple forms) –
would conditional clauses – indirect questions –
relatives with *where/when* – gerunds after prepositions/phrases …

I was glad. Now Hyde could not show his face to the world
again. If he did, every honest man in London would be proud
to report him to the police. ***Dr Jekyll and Mr Hyde***

… future continuous – future perfect –
passive (modals, continuous forms) –
would have conditional clauses – modals + perfect infinitive …

If he had spoken Estella's name, I would have hit him. I was so
angry with him, and so depressed about my future, that I could
not eat the breakfast. Instead I went straight to the old house.
Great Expectations

… passive (infinitives, gerunds) – advanced modal meanings –
clauses of concession, condition

When I stepped up to the piano, I was confident. It was as if I
knew that the prodigy side of me really did exist. And when I
started to play, I was so caught up in how lovely I looked that
I didn't worry how I would sound. ***The Joy Luck Club***

Much Ado About Nothing

WILLIAM SHAKESPEARE

Retold by Alistair McCallum

There are two love stories in this fast-moving comedy.

Brave young Claudio and Leonato's pretty daughter Hero are in love and want to marry, but Don John has a wicked plan to stop their wedding. Will he succeed, or will the truth come out? Will Claudio and Hero marry, after all?

Beatrice and Benedick are always arguing with each other, but how do they really feel? Perhaps they are more interested in each other than they seem to be! Their friends work hard to bring them closer together.

One Thousand Dollars and Other Plays

O. HENRY

Retold by John Escott

Money or love? Which is more important in life? Can money buy anything? Can it help a young man to marry the girl he loves? Does money really make people happy, or does it just cause problems?

We all know how difficult love can be. When you meet someone you like, there are so many things that can go wrong, sometimes because you are trying too hard, sometimes because of a misunderstanding.

These four plays about money, love and life are adapted from short stories written a hundred years ago by the great American storyteller O. Henry. Henry had his own difficulties with money and loneliness, and wrote from personal experience.